In Memory

Of

Mary Jane Nagel

© 1987 GAYLORD

HEINEMANN Profiles

Diana

Princess of Wales

An Unauthorized Biography

Haydn Middleton

Heinemann Library
Des Plaines, Illinois

© 1999 Reed Educational & Professional PublishingPublished by Heinemann Library,an imprint of Reed Educational & Professional Publishing,1350 East Touhy Avenue, Suite 240 West Des Plaines, IL 60018

Designed by Visual Image
Printed in Hong Kong / China

03 02 01 00 99

10 9 8 7 6 5 4 3 2 1

Library of Congress Cataloging-in-Publication Data
Middleton, Haydn
    Diana, Princess of Wales / Haydn Middleton.
        p.   cm. - - (Heinemann profiles.)
    Includes bibliographical references and index.
    Summary: Follows the background, family life, publice image, humanitarian work, death, and influences of the woman who married Prince Charles of England.
      ISBN 1-57572-716-1 (lib. bdg.)
      1. Diana, Princess of Wales, 1961-1997--Juvenile literature.
    2. Princesses--Great Britain--Biography--Juvenile literature.
    [1. Diana, Princess of Wales, 1961-1997. 2. Princesses. 3. Women--Biography.] 1. Title. II. Series.
    DA591.A45D5344 1998
    941.085'092--dc21
    [B]   98-23294
                                      CIP
                                      AC

Acknowledgments
The Publishers would like to thank the following for permission to reproduce photographs: AP pp. 40, 43; Camera Press p. 5; L. Cherruault pp. 18, 21; S. Dinukanovic p. 6; K. Goff pp. 30, 33; LNS p. 13; PA/RBO pp. 7, 8; K. Rand p. 19; T. Wood p. 24; Chris Honeywell pp. 34, 38; Hulton-Deutsch Collection p14; Mirror Group Newspapers p. 36; PA News Photo Library p32; Press Association p12; Rex Features, London pp. 10, 16, 22, 23, 26, 42; P. Brooker p. 28; P. Nichols p. 25; T. Rooke pp. 4, 41, 50; C Sykes p. 29; The Sun p. 35; Sygma p. 47; BBC Panorama p. 39; A. Murry p. 44, M. Polak p. 49.

Cover photograph reproduced with permission of Camera Press.
Every effort has been made to contact copyright holders of any material reproduced in this book. Any omissions will be rectified in subsequent printings if notice is given to the Publisher.

Any words appearing in the text in bold, **like this,** are explained in the Glossary.

*Grand Rapids 4/99 $16.00 31570
Learning Source*

CONTENTS

WHO WAS DIANA?

Britain, unlike many countries, still has a royal family. During the late 1990s, its members were the subject of a big public debate. Should they stay remote from the people they ruled over or try to be more like them? Should they keep to traditional ways or adopt a modern style of rule?

The life of Diana, Princess of Wales (1961–1997), contributed greatly to this debate. Born into the English **upper class**, in 1981 she married Queen Elizabeth II's son and **heir** Charles **Windsor**, the Prince of Wales. For the next 16 years Diana was rarely out of the news. Her image appeared in countless magazines. Her work for charity and other good causes was reported at length, and so, more controversially, were the details of her private life. She became one of the world's best-known women, and many believed her to be one of the most beautiful.

Diana seemed relaxed and natural, even on formal occasions.

Queen Elizabeth II invented the royal walkabout, but Diana perfected this informal way of meeting the people.

Diana's style was emotional and outspoken. This pleased people who wanted the **monarchy** to appear more up to date. Others felt that by seeming so "ordinary," Diana lowered the royal family's dignity. Her tragic death in a car accident, when she was only 36 years old, caused millions of people worldwide to **mourn** her—and to debate even more fiercely what kind of a monarchy Britain should have.

A Privileged Background

Diana's father, Edward John Spencer, married her mother, Frances Ruth Burke Roche, in 1953. Both of them belonged to the British **upper class**.

For generations, the head of Diana's family has held the important title of earl Spencer. When a British earl dies, his title passes to his oldest son, along with his land, his wealth and the ancestral home, the family's inherited house. Earls also still help to govern Britain, as members of the House of Lords in **Parliament**.

Althorp House is the ancestral home of the Spencer family.

THE NEED FOR A SON AND HEIR

The Spencers are very proud of their history and traditions. They are linked by blood to King Charles II and to U.S. President George Washington. Their ancestral home is Althorp House in Northamptonshire. When Diana was born, her grandfather was the seventh earl Spencer. After his death, Diana's father would become the eighth earl, but until then he was called Viscount Althorp.

A NEW EARL IS BORN

Diana's parents wanted a son who would one day become the ninth Earl Spencer. But their first two children, born six and four years before Diana, were daughters: Sarah and Jane. Then, on July 1, 1961, came Diana herself. "I was the girl who was supposed to be a boy," she remarked later, and although her parents loved her, she often felt that she had disappointed them. Luckily, in 1964, a baby boy was born: Charles.

Diana, age seven, with her younger brother Charles in 1968.

CHILDHOOD CHANGES

Diana was on horseback by the age of three and soon came to love all animals.

Diana grew up at Park House in Norfolk. This was close to one of the royal family's homes, at Sandringham. Sometimes Diana and her brother Charles played with Andrew and Edward, the two younger sons of Queen Elizabeth II. Once Diana went to watch the movie *Chitty Chitty Bang Bang* at Sandringham's private theater.

A BROKEN FAMILY

In 1967, when Diana was six, her parents separated. Eventually they were divorced and both of them went on to marry again. Diana and the other children found this very difficult. They still saw their mother, but continued to live with their father. A series of nannies took care of them when they were not away at **boarding school**. (It is usual for the children of upper class families to go away to school.)

From the age of six, Diana went first to Riddlesworth Hall in Norfolk and then to West Heath in Kent. Although she was not unhappy at these schools, she later recalled, "I always felt very detached from everyone else. I knew I was going somewhere different, that I was in the wrong shell."

THE MOVE TO ALTHORP

In 1975 Diana's grandfather died, and her father became the eighth Earl Spencer. The family moved from Park House to the ancestral home at Althorp, a rambling house full of scary corners and stern-looking family portraits.

As an Earl's daughter, Diana herself was now called "Lady" Diana. But she still had to go to school like any other teenage girl. Her progress there was slow. She was a talented diver and dancer, but she left West Heath school without graduating.

SWITZERLAND AND LONDON

After Diana left "finishing school," she worked at a nursery school taking care of young children.

In 1977 Diana, like her sister before her, went to a finishing school in Switzerland. This was a place where girls from rich families were taught the finer points of cooking and sewing, and learned to speak fluent French. Diana disliked it and came back to England after only six weeks.

GETTING STARTED

During the next three years, the Spencer family's wealth proved very useful. Diana was given her own apartment in London's Earl's Court, where she lived with two close friends. (The words "Chief Chick" were stuck to her bedroom door, just to show who was the boss.) She did not have to earn her living, so she took whatever jobs appealed to her. Usually these involved young children. She worked as a nanny and also helped the teachers at the Young England Kindergarten School, in London's Pimlico district.

AN ORDINARY KIND OF GIRL

By the age of 19, Diana was a tall, shy, likable young woman. Like most people her age, she enjoyed dancing, partying, and watching television. Her family and friends jokingly called her "Duchess" or "Duch," but, unlike some privileged young people, she did not seem snobbish or proud.

She had a taste for practical jokes. With her friend Carolyn Bartholomew, she spent quiet evenings reading through the telephone book and calling people with silly names. Once they covered a friend's Alfa Romeo car in eggs and flour, which set like concrete. She had plenty of friends who were boys, but until she was almost 20, she had no steady boyfriend. That was about to change.

THE ROYAL CONNECTION

Back in November 1977, Diana went to a weekend party in a country house. One of the people there was the Queen's oldest son, Charles **Windsor**, the Prince of Wales and **heir** to the throne. Diana had known the Prince as a child, but not very well—he was 12 years older than she, and lately Diana had thought of him only as her sister Sarah's friend.

CHARLES NOTICES DIANA

That weekend, Charles noticed Diana. Later he remembered her as "a very jolly, amusing, and attractive 16 year old, full of fun."

At Caernarfon Castle, North Wales, in 1969, Queen Elizabeth II formally proclaimed her son Charles "Prince of Wales."

As time passed, they got to know each other better, even though Diana still had to call him "Sir," because there are strict rules about how to address a Prince.

A ROYAL ROMANCE?

In mid–1980 rumors began to spread that Charles and Diana were about to get engaged. So many **media** reporters pestered Diana to know the truth that her mother wrote an angry letter to *The Times* newspaper about the misery they were causing. Then on February 24, 1981, the world was let in on the secret. It was announced that Charles, now 31, and Diana, 19, were to marry. One TV interviewer asked them if they were in love. "Of course," answered Diana. "Whatever 'in love' means," added Charles.

Prince Charles and Lady Diana became engaged in 1981.

May I ask the editors of Fleet Street, whether, in the execution of their jobs, they consider it necessary or fair to harass my daughter daily, from dawn until well after dusk? Is it fair to ask any human being, regardless of circumstances, to be treated in this way?
Diana's mother's letter to *The Times,* December 1980

A New Royal Couple

This photograph
of the royal
family was taken
in 1977.
Although the
poses look
somewhat stiff,
this was seen as
quite an
informal
photograph
at the time.

After the announcement, Diana moved out of her apartment. First she moved into Clarence House, the Queen Mother's London home, then into Buckingham Palace. There she was better protected from the **media** reporters and photographers, who still flocked to see her night and day.

The challenge ahead

The wedding was planned for July 29, 1981. Massive preparations had to be made for this huge public event. Diana also had to prepare herself for becoming the first Princess of Wales in 71 years (and only the ninth in all of British history). After July 29, she would be the third most important woman in Great Britain, after only the Queen and the Queen Mother. How was the former kindergarten helper going to cope? What, exactly, would she be expected to *do*?

The duties of a princess

First and foremost, she would have to give birth to a male **heir** for Prince Charles, a son who would one day become King himself. (Diana knew all about sons and heirs from her own family upbringing.) She would also have to accompany Charles on his various appearances in Britain and overseas. Sometimes she would have to appear on her own, and serve as **patron** or president of a number of organizations like, for example, the Welsh National Opera or the Royal School for the Blind.

The center of attention

In addition to her public duties, Diana would have to deal with men and women from the media. The British royal family already fascinated millions. As its newest and prettiest member, Diana would be sure to attract a lot of attention, at least until people got used to her. Then, Buckingham Palace officials hoped, the fuss would die down.

Charles and
Diana share in
the crowd's
enthusiasm and
joy on the day
of the royal
wedding.

As her wedding approached, Diana began almost visibly to shrink under the pressures. Her waist measurement fell from 28.9 in. (73.5cm) at her engagement to 22.8 in. (58cm) on July 29. But when the great day arrived, she disappointed no one as she walked up the long aisle of St. Paul's Cathedral on the arm of her father. Coming up to the Prince's side, she looked radiant in her dress of ivory silk taffeta with its long train.

THE STUFF OF FAIRY TALES?

A congregation of 2,500 people watched Diana marry Charles. A further 750 million shared in the event on television. At the time, it was the biggest worldwide audience ever recorded. The Archbishop of Canterbury, who married the couple, was inspired like many of the onlookers. He remarked that the marriage was "the stuff of which fairy tales are made."

The fairy tale continued as the newlyweds enjoyed a long honeymoon, which included a Mediterranean cruise on the royal yacht *Britannia*. Then Charles and Diana took up residence in their two new homes: Kensington Palace in London and Highgrove House in Gloucester. Twelve days before the wedding, Diana had written in a private letter, "In 12 days' time I shall no longer be me." But even she could not have guessed what a world **celebrity** she would become.

Meeting the People

Charles and Diana's first royal engagement was a three-day, 435-mile (700-kilometer) tour of Wales. Thousands of people lined the streets, and most of them made it clear who they had come to see.

The public reacts to Diana

If Charles walked on one side of the street during a **walkabout**, the crowds would groan because his fairy-tale princess was too far away on the other. "I'm sorry," Charles would joke, "I don't have enough wives to go around." This was just the beginning. Similar scenes would soon be repeated all over the world.

In the early years of her marriage, Diana seemed camera shy.

DIANA LEARNS TO CHARM THE PUBLIC

Diana had always been quite shy with strangers. Now it was part of her job to appear before large crowds of them. She was also expected to talk briefly with some of them, to ask questions, and to make comments. This did not come naturally to her. Even at school, she had agreed to act in a play only if she had a nonspeaking part. But people were charmed by the obvious efforts she was making, and the **media's** interest in her grew. The attention became greater than it had been before the wedding.

Diana attracted crowds of photographers whatever the occasion.

This interest reached a new intensity on November 5, 1981. On that day, it was officially announced that Princess Diana was pregnant.

Becoming a Mother

Diana's baby was due to be born in June 1982, but she kept up her public duties until the end of March. Often she felt terribly tired and she suffered, like many mothers-to-be, from bouts of sickness. It did not help to be constantly watched by photographers and to have every move she made reported in the newspapers.

A plea for privacy

Unknown to Diana, the British newspapers' editors were called to Buckingham Palace. There the Queen's **press secretary** asked them to give the Princess a little more privacy. They ignored the request. In the modern world, if the public wants information about a person, the **media** will seek to supply it. And the appetite for information about Diana was growing all the time.

In February 1982 a private vacation in the Bahamas was upset by photographs of the Princess published in two British papers. Large sums of money changed hands for their **syndication** round the world. The photographs of the pregnant princess wearing a bikini had naturally been taken without either her knowledge or consent.

British *Daily Telegraph,* September 1, 1997
(obituary)

Prince William went with Prince Charles and Princess Diana on their tour of Australia and New Zealand in 1982. Diana wanted her children to spend as much time with their parents as possible.

A SON AND HEIR

On June 21, 1982, ten days before her 21st birthday, Diana gave birth to a baby boy, William. "Thank goodness," said the delighted Queen, "he hasn't got ears like his father." At once little Prince William became the **heir-apparent** to the British throne. Before he was one year old, he went with his parents on a long official tour of Australia and New Zealand. Later in 1983, Charles and Diana toured another **Commonwealth** country, Canada.

No one had ever seen such enthusiastic welcomes for members of the royal family. But, as in Britain, the star of the show was obviously Diana. "I'm only here to collect the flowers," smiled Prince Charles.

FAMILY LIFE

O n September 15, 1984, Diana gave birth to a second son. He was christened Henry, but she announced that he would be known as Harry. An important part of her job as Princess of Wales had now been done. As the old saying goes, she had produced "an **heir** and a spare."

A LOVING MOTHER

Although Diana found it hard to live in the **media** spotlight, motherhood came more easily to her. She lavished love and attention on her sons as they grew up. Two such boys could never hope to lead normal lives. But Diana made sure that they had fun at theme parks and pizza restaurants, along with the more solemn future public duties.

Princes William and Harry performing their public role as members of the royal family.

The young
Princes enjoyed
a fun outing at
a theme park
with their
mother.

THE STRAIN BEGINS TO SHOW

Diana's popularity soared even higher when she
showed herself to be a caring mother. By tradition,
the royal family behaved in a **formal**, seemingly
unfeeling way. Many people, especially women,
thought that Diana's openly emotional style made a
very welcome change.

But behind the happy family smiles, all was not well.
The stress of being Princess of Wales was making
Diana ill. Often she looked painfully thin, and in
later years she admitted that she had suffered not
only from postnatal depression but also from the
eating disorder known as **bulimia nervosa**. Adored
from afar by millions, she felt more and more cut off
from the real world. But there was no way for her to
express her worries. Members of the royal family
were expected to have a "stiff upper lip" and not
show what they really felt.

PATRON AND PRESIDENT

In spite of her health problems, Diana had to carry out a number of duties which went with the job of being a member of the royal family. Some of these were, by tradition, military. She was, for example, Colonel in Chief of the Royal Hampshire Regiment, and Honorary Air Commodore of RAF Wittering. She took her military **roles** seriously. In December 1990, during the Gulf War, Diana traveled to Germany to visit the families of British troops serving in the Middle East.

Part of Diana's work for charities included making speeches and talking to the public about this part of her job.

THE BUSY CHARITY WORKER

Diana also gave her name, as **patron** or president, of many different organizations, ranging from the National Children's Orchestra to the Pre-School Playgroups Association and Help the Aged.

She served these organizations not just as a figurehead but as a fund raiser, a chair of meetings and a spokeswoman.

AN INVOLVED PATRON

Passionate about ballet as a child, Diana was an extremely strong patron of the Royal Ballet Company.

Gradually she overcame her shyness to become an effective and sincere public speaker. She took a close personal interest in whatever organization she was involved with. When she became patron of the British Deaf Association, for instance, she learned sign language and frequently used it in public. Thus she brought a very human touch to her work as a Princess.

A Love Affair
with the Camera

When Diana became engaged to Prince Charles, she was pretty in a girl-next-door kind of way. That was one reason why she immediately became so popular. To many of her female fans, she seemed like one of them.

Diana knew how to make the most of her appearance, but she wanted to be seen as more than a mere beauty.

But in the years after her marriage, Diana's good looks turned into movie-star-like beauty. This proved to be a mixed blessing for her.

A MEDIA OBSESSION

During the 1980s, the **media** became obsessed with her weight and appearance. There were regular comments about her slim figure. Few people knew that this was a result of her illness. Most simply marveled at her glamour. In appearance at least, she was no longer "one of us," but a dazzling **icon** and inspiration.

THE "ROYAL CLOTHES HORSE"

The Princess made a huge impact on the world of fashion. British clothes designers like the Emanuels, who made her wedding dress, became even more popular after she was photographed wearing their outfits. And Diana never seemed to look less than perfect in a photograph, even when she was snapped off duty, as she often was. It was almost as if she had been created for the camera.

But behind the goddesslike image, there was a real person—and this person felt that her life was far from perfect. "She was expected by the royal system to be a clothes horse and an obedient wife," one of her advisers said later. Yet Diana now wanted, as she herself put it, "to do, not just to be."

A New Direction

In 1988 Diana reached a turning point in her life. During a skiing holiday at Klosters in Switzerland, Major Hugh Lindsay, a friend of Prince Charles, was killed in an accident. For a while, it was feared that Charles might have died too. The shock made Diana think hard about her own life and how she could change it for the better.

Setting her own agenda

She decided to seek medical help for her eating disorder. She began a new fitness regimen with the advice of a trainer. With regard to her public work, she concentrated on helping those who were seriously disadvantaged, neglected, or dying from diseases like AIDS and leprosy.

Diana gladly gave her time to causes that she felt strongly about.

MEETING MOTHER THERESA

In 1991 she made seven visits to hostels for the
homeless. In 1992 she met with Mother Teresa of
Calcutta, whose aim was to help the poorest of the
poor. Diana's interest in health issues gave her less
time for her other interests. "There are more
important things in life than ballet," she explained.
"There are people dying on the streets."

Her concern for the less fortunate was genuine. It
won her praise from the **media** and public alike. But
as Mother Teresa had told her, "To heal other people,
you have to suffer yourself." And only Diana's closest
friends knew how much she was suffering.

ANCIENT VERSUS MODERN

Diana's
sister-in-law,
Sarah Ferguson,
Duchess of York,
(left) was
another modern
young woman
who found it
hard to fit into
the royal family's
traditions.

Diana could seek treatment for her illness, but there was another problem for which there seemed to be no cure. She had never felt truly comfortable as a member of the royal family.

Usually when outsiders married into the **Windsor** family, they quickly learned how to act royal in public and in private. Diana was different. She liked to be spontaneous and easygoing, cuddling and kissing her sons in public, even hugging the patients on her hospital visits.

The Queen and her relatives, including Prince Charles, had been trained to behave in a less hands-on way, and with somewhat more **pomp** and ceremony. For as long as anyone could remember, this had been the British tradition.

TIME FOR A CHANGE?

But by the 1990s, as traditions changed elsewhere in British life, the royal family began to look old-fashioned to some people. Others asked why there had to be a **monarchy** at all. Most other countries no longer had kings or queens. If they did, as in the Netherlands and Sweden, their kings and queens behaved in a much less formal way. For example, they rode bicycles instead of being driven in horse-drawn carriages.

Diana believed that the British royal family had to appear more up to date if it were to stay popular with the British people. Sadly for her, Prince Charles did not fully agree. In some ways, he was right to disagree. In 1986, his brother Prince Andrew, the Duke of York, married a lively young woman named Sarah Ferguson. "Fergie," the new Duchess of York, saw no reason to speak or act in a stuffy royal way. At first she was welcomed by the **media** and the public as a breath of fresh air. But soon her breezy style came under fire, and she was fiercely criticized for not being formal enough.

Eagle-eyed photographers pounced on public moments like this, when Carles and Diana had uncomfortable moments.

Around 1990, there were rumors that Diana and Charles were having other disagreements too. When they went on official visits abroad, the **media** searched for telltale signs that they were no longer happy in each other's company. There were whispers that their marriage had broken up, that both of them had turned to new relationships.

No one could be sure exactly what was happening between them. In a sense it was nobody's business but their own. But Charles and Diana had been in the media spotlight for so long that no part of their lives seemed private any more. This only added to the royal couple's problems. It can often be hard to make even normal marriages work, as Diana's own parents had discovered. But when millions of people are constantly watching, it can become almost impossible.

Diana posed, wistful and alone at the Taj Mahal, a great romantic monument, in 1992.

SEPARATION

In March 1992, there was a royal sensation. It was announced that the marriage of the Queen's son had broken up, and that he and his wife were going to separate. The son was Prince Andrew, his wife the Duchess of York. Certain sections of the **media** predicted that the next royal marriage to fail would be Charles and Diana's, and soon.

THE BOMBSHELL BOOK

In mid-1992, *The Sunday Times* newspaper began to print parts of a new book. *Diana: Her True Story* was written by a journalist named Andrew Morton. The author had spoken to Diana's close friends, learned how unhappy she was, and then described her married life in detail. Some readers, mistrusting the media, thought it was all untrue. The **Press Complaints Commission** condemned both author and newspaper for "dabbling their fingers in the stuff of other people's souls."

DIANA

Her True Story

Including a new chapter and 28 new photographs

ANDREW MORTON

A STARTLING REVELATION

But then Diana made a very public visit to someone who had helped Morton to write the book. This was a signal that, in a way, Diana herself had cooperated with the author. (Five years later, Morton revealed that Diana had actually read and corrected his text before the book was published.) The story —or at least Diana's side of it—was therefore, true.

After the separation, Diana appeared to enjoy herself more at public functions.

Thus it came as no surprise when, in December 1992, Prime Minister John Major announced in **Parliament** that Charles and Diana had jointly decided to separate. The fairy tale was over.

BIRTH-DI DATE AT THE TATE

Arty party . . Lady Helen Taylor and hubby Tim   Di-ing to see her . . Viscount Linley and Serena

The Sun GOES TO THE BIG ROYAL PARTY

PRINCESS Di dazzles celebrities as she steps out last night in a stunning low-cut dress to celebrate her birthday.

By WAYNE FRANCIS, Royal Reporter, and BEN PROCTOR

The Princess was 36 yesterday — and looked fabulous in a sleek full-length black evening gown as she arrived for a glittering gala.

A crowd had gathered outside London's Tate Gallery to catch a glimpse of Di — and cheered when they saw her in the £2,500 outfit, created by top designer Jacques Azaguri.

Di joined her brother Lord Spencer and a host of stars and pals for the champagne

Attenborough — who arrived in a gold Rolls-Royce.

Also there were Lady Helen Taylor and her husband Tim, Viscount Linley and wife Serena, singer Bryan Ferry with his wife Lucy, and David Bowie's supermodel wife Iman.

Di was greeted by gallery boss Nicholas Serota – a controversial figure in the British art world – as she arrived.

Favourite

More than 500 guests attended the £350-a-head reception among the Tate's

fillet of sea bass and a strawberry and cream dessert called Eton Mess — washed down with vintage wine.

Di shared a table and a joke with Lord Hindlip – the man who caused a stir last week when cameras seemed to catch him putting his hand on her bottom.

But this time Christie's boss Lord Hindlip – who auctioned Di's gowns in New York and raised £3.5million for charity – kept his arm firmly around the waist of Lady Hindlip.

The gala evening, sponsored by Chanel, was expected to raise £200,000 for the Tate's redevelopment appeal.

Controversial artist Damien Hirst, best known for his exhibits of pickled sheep and butchered cow, was asked

PRINCESS ON THE RUN

Charles and Diana had no immediate plans to divorce. They set up separate households at Kensington Palace and Highgrove House, then continued to carry out their public duties apart.

STILL IN THE PUBLIC EYE

The **media's** interest in them both did not die down. It published intimate details of their other friendships after paying for tapes of **tapped** telephone calls. In November 1993, secretly-taken photos were printed showing Diana exercising in a London gym.

HOLIDAY DIANA GETS IN THE SWIM AS SHE REJECTS SECURITY RISK ACCUSATION

I'VE DONE NOTHING SARONG

From JAMES WHITAKER in St Tropez

Playing safe but sexy

By HELEN WEATHERS

ON A WAVE: Daredevil Harry aboard a jet ski

HIGH FLIER: Princess Diana leaps aboard the Cujo yesterday and, inset, shares a cuddle with son Harry – it was all very relaxed but

SHY: Wills shields his face as Di he

Whatever she did—comforting a dying child, speaking on behalf of a charity, or simply buying balloons in a toy shop—she was front-page news.

The media turns negative

In addition, report after report was written about the Princess's health and state of mind. Often these were ill informed, sometimes they were cruel. Certain reporters now spoke harshly about her, calling her a schemer, someone who used the media to put across her own messages but then blamed the same media for all her troubles.

For a year from December 1993, Diana tried to withdraw from public life as much as possible to win some time and space for herself and her sons. Even so, the stories and rumors about her did not end. The media was particularly interested in her new male friends, and also in a female friend of Prince Charles, Camilla Parker-Bowles.

> Diana's shyness was one of her most misleading character traits. It is not the bashfulness of youth, but the statement of her whole style of operating… [She] did not pause to analyze … her own appeal, but she knew how to use it. That's why she began her extraordinary physical transformation from mouse to movie star.
>
> *Vanity Fair*, October 1985

TELLING ALL ON TELEVISION

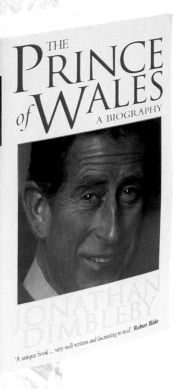

As a result of the breakdown of Charles and Diana's marriage, the royal family received some bad publicity. In mid-1994, Prince Charles tried to show his human side by helping Jonathan Dimbleby to make a television **documentary** about himself. But during the television interview, he practically admitted that he had been unfaithful to Diana. The newspapers made it clear that his unnamed love interest was his old friend, Mrs. Camilla Parker-Bowles.

Jonathan Dimbleby's 1994 television documentary about Charles was accompanied by a more detailed book about the Prince.

"We were told when we got engaged that the **media** would go quietly," Diana said on *Panorama*, "and it didn't, and then when we were married they said it would go quietly and it didn't; and then it started very much to focus on me, and I seemed to be on the front of a newspaper every single day, which is an isolating experience." As for the future, she said, "I would like to be a Queen in people's hearts ... someone's got to go out there and love people."   November 20, 1995

Diana wanted the public to understand her point of view and gave an interview that was broadcast on television.

The next year, Diana arranged for her own hour-long interview on BBC TV's current affairs program "Panorama." Her aim was finally to tell the truth about her years as a member of the royal family. She spoke openly about her unhappiness, an affair with Major James Hewitt, her love for her children, and her devotion to her public work.

Millions of people around the world were touched or shocked, depending on their view of the Princess. This interview, like Charles's, certainly affected the way that people saw the **monarchy** and made them think hard about how they felt the members of the royal family should behave.

DIVORCE AND AFTER

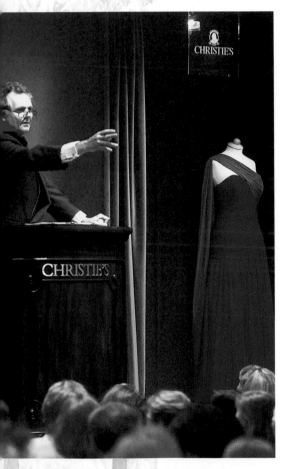

An evening gown of Princess Diana's is auctioned in New York to raise money for charity.

Four weeks after Diana's "Panorama" interview, the Queen wrote to Charles and Diana and advised them to divorce. It seemed to her that this was now the only way forward. The couple agreed, and on August 28, 1996, their divorce became final. They were given joint **custody** of their sons, and both parents continued to play a large part in raising them.

"PRINCESS OF THE WORLD"

Diana had lost the title of Her Royal Highness, but a new **role** beckoned. "I see myself as a princess for the world," she had once said, "not the Princess of Wales." She wished to use her fame to do good on a global scale. As if to make a new start, in July 1997 she auctioned off 79 designer dresses in New York to raise money for the charities closest to her heart. Her son William was said to have given her the idea.

FIGHTING LAND MINES

She also threw herself into supporting the work of the Red Cross. In particular, she took a leading part in its international campaign to ban antipersonnel land mines.

These weapons killed around 800 people every month and wounded or handicapped a further 1,200, many of them civilians, including women and children.

By visiting battle zones in Angola and Bosnia, Diana drew attention to the land mines' brutal effect. "It was not until the Princess became involved," said the Director General of the British Red Cross, "that everyone woke up to this problem. Millions of people around the world saw her talking about the issue."

Diana became a strong and active supporter of the anti–land mine charities and visited countries, like Angola, in this photograph, where land mine accidents happen.

DEATH IN PARIS

During the 1990s, public interest in Diana's love life reached fever pitch. The **media speculated** endlessly about who her current boyfriend might be. Millions of words were written and broadcast about whom she might marry next. And hundreds of photographs were printed of the Princess off duty, in the company of various male friends.

Diana gives a clear signal to press photographers.

A picture from a security camera in the Ritz Hotel shows Diana and Dodi Al-Fayed, who has his arm around the Princess, just before the fatal accident.

`00:19:23 3      /97 12HR`

AN UNWELCOME PRESENCE

Many of these snapshots were taken by international photographers known as paparazzi, Italian slang for "swarming insects." For years the paparazzi had been buzzing around world-famous **celebrities**, taking unwelcome photos, then selling them to the magazine or newspaper that paid them the most money. Diana, like many modern stars, claimed that their attention was **intrusive** and annoying.

THE FINAL JOURNEY

Paparazzi on motorcycles were following a car carrying the Princess in the early hours of the morning of August 31, 1997. She was spending the weekend in Paris with a new friend, wealthy Egyptian Dodi Al-Fayed. Their speeding car ran out of control in a tunnel. In the crash that followed, the driver and Al-Fayed were killed instantly. A British bodyguard was saved, and Diana was removed from the wreckage. But she was too severely injured to survive. At the age of 36, she died in the hospital.

The Floral Revolution

No one was quite prepared for what came next. While Prince Charles and Diana's two sisters flew to Paris to claim her body, a large part of the world's population found itself deeply shaken by her death.

Grief strikes a nation

In Britain, where by tradition people were expected not to show emotion at difficult times, there was an open display of grief. The airwaves, newspapers, and new internet sites were filled with tributes to the Princess, reports on the tragedy, and discussions of how she would be remembered.

Floral tributes were left in front of Kensington Palace in memory of Diana, Princess of Wales.

THE PEOPLE MOURN

There were also many interviews with ordinary members of the public, who had gone out onto the streets to express their sorrow and respect. Thousands of **mourners** made their way to Kensington and Buckingham Palaces. Outside the gates, they left a sea of flowers accompanied by heartfelt messages of love and sadness. Many stood in line for up to 12 hours to sign the **Books of Condolence**.

Most of these people had never met the Princess. But, like her, they were following their emotions. "I work by instinct," Diana had told a French reporter in June 1997, "that's my best adviser." The instinct of millions of British people told them that they had lost someone unique.

College lecturers John and Ellen Baglow traveled by train to London from Somerset. "It's a bit embarrassing really," said John. "This isn't the sort of behavior you expect from a lecturer. But I had to be there to pay my respects. Somehow it was an important gesture. I don't quite know why." Ellen added, "I'm not a person who likes to show my emotions. I prefer to grieve in private. But when I knew the rest of the family was coming, I wanted to be with them." *Observer* September 7, 1997

"A Queen in People's Hearts"

"I'm not a political animal," Diana once said, "but I think the biggest disease this world suffers from in this day and age is the disease of feeling unloved, and I know that I can give love for a minute, for half an hour, for a day, for a month. But I can give, and I'm very happy to do that, and I want to do that." At her funeral on September 6, 1997, few could doubt that very deep feelings were now felt for her in return.

LAST RITES

Over a million people lined the route that her coffin was carried along, from Kensington Palace to Westminster Abbey. The procession took place in almost total silence, apart from the clicking of camera shutters.

The funeral service featured traditional hymns and prayers, but a more modern note was struck with "Candle in the Wind," a tribute song from Diana's pop-star friend Elton John. Diana's younger brother Charles, now the ninth Earl Spencer, spoke lovingly of his dead sister. He also bitterly attacked the **media** for giving her so little privacy, and even seemed to criticize the royal family's traditional formality.

THE WORLD WATCHES

The service was watched by over 31 million television viewers in Britain. BBC TV transmitted it live to 187 countries too. In death as in life, Diana was the center of global attention. Diana's body was then driven away to be buried on a small island on the grounds of Althorp, the Spencers' ancestral home. In modern times, no member of the British royal family has ever had so strong an effect on the hearts and minds of so many people.

How People Saw Diana

On the day before Diana's funeral, Queen Elizabeth II made a television broadcast. She said "No one who knew Diana will ever forget her. Millions of others who never met her, but felt they knew her, will remember her." Most people's impressions of Diana were formed by the **media**. For 17 years, she was very big news. During that time, the media presented her in several different ways: as a devoted mother and a glamorous jet setter; as a typically modern woman and an old-fashioned housewife; as a tireless charity worker and a self-pitying moaner. This was partly because, at different times, she *was* all these things.

One of her closest friends, Rosa Monckton, wrote: "Diana had such a conflict of personalities within one character. She was complicated on the one hand and simple and naive on the other. These two existed together, sometimes awkwardly, and made her life more difficult than it should have been."

Diana: for and against

From 1980 to 1997, Diana's public image was constantly changing, as different parts of her character became clear. As a 19 year old, she seemed shy, sweet, and nervous. Gradually she became more relaxed and confident, and people began to see her warm, emotional nature.

Diana was especially popular with women. She shared the interests and worries of less wealthy women, and she spoke from the heart about them. This seemed to give her a common touch, which other members of the royal family clearly lacked.

But she did not convince everyone. Some journalists, representing another section of public opinion, called her empty headed and childish. They resented the amount of attention given to her and suspected that she herself thrived on it, even when the attention was critical.

In 1992, British journalist Julie Burchill described Diana as "...our Pop Princess... . She is Madonna crossed with Mother Teresa, a glorious totem of Western ideals."

These critics grew weary of her complaints about her unhappiness and said that she was unrealistic for ever having believed in a fairy tale romance with Charles. Some of them thought there was no longer a need for a **monarchy** at all. Others believed that if there was still to be a royal family, its members had to go on showing the traditional dignity and formality. A common touch was exactly what was *not* needed.

Diana's effect on the monarchy

Most people's opinions of Diana were really opinions of her image in the **media**. Some believed that she carefully shaped this image herself. Others believed that the image shaped her, until finally she had to cry for help by helping Andrew Morton to write his biography and by giving the "Panorama" television interview.

Whatever the truth is, for better or worse the media's obsession with Diana changed people's ideas about the monarchy. Some of these ideas could not be ignored, even by the Queen. On October 17, 1997, the newspaper *The Times* carried this story:

> The Queen has accepted that the Royal Family must change its image after the death of Diana, Princess of Wales.... There will be no sudden switch of style, but a source close to the Queen spoke yesterday of the need to demonstrate "softer, gentler touches" in the wake of what he described as the first royal tragedy to occur in the mass media culture.

The older **Windsors** may find it hard to show these "softer, gentler touches." This may lead more people than ever to ask if the royal family still has a purpose to serve. But the monarchy has proved to be successful at surviving periods of unpopularity in the past (see next page). By adapting itself to the new public mood, it will probably continue well into the twenty-first century.

CROWN AND PEOPLE— THE LONG VIEW

In 1981, Diana became part of a **monarchy** that had existed for 1,500 years. Until around 1700, kings and queens paid little attention to public relations. They expected their subjects to obey them, not to have opinions about them. But as **Parliament** gradually took over the day-to-day running of the country, Britain's monarchs and their families became more like figureheads. In that **role**, they were expected to behave in a dignified way and to set a good example for the public.

WAS THE MONARCHY ALWAYS POPULAR?

Some monarchs were better figureheads than others. George III (1760–1820) went mad toward the end of his long reign. George IV (1820–30) was regularly attacked in newspaper articles for his lavish style of life when times were hard for his people. William IV (1830–37) had no fewer than 15 illegitimate children.

Queen Victoria (1837–1901), with her husband Prince Albert, helped to restore some dignity to the monarchy. But public opinion turned against her, too, when she hid herself away after Albert's death. After the brief reign of Edward VII (1901–10), George V (1910–36) came closer to his people by making radio broadcasts every Christmas.

A serious, down-to-earth man, George V made himself more popular still by presenting the trophy at the football Cup Final at Wembley. But in 1936, the less dutiful Edward VIII (1936) gave up his throne to marry a woman whom his advisers believed to be unsuitable. Then George VI (1936–52) won respect by helping to raise the nation's morale during World War II.

MEETING THE PEOPLE'S EXPECTATIONS

The relationship between the British people and its royal families has had many ups and downs. The current queen, Elizabeth II (1952–), has remained personally popular, but her family has been widely criticized for behaving in an unsuitable way.

Princess Diana once said that she wanted "to do, not just to be." Being just a figurehead was not enough for her. But it is difficult to know exactly what the British want their royal family to do, at the end of the twentieth century. Suitable behavior means different things to different people, as was clearly shown by the widely differing public responses to the career of Diana herself.

Diana, Princess of Wales—Timeline

1961	(July 1) Diana born as third daughter of the future Earl Spencer
1981	(February 24) Official announcement of Diana's engagement to be married to Prince Charles
1981	(July 29) Marriage to Prince Charles in St. Paul's Cathedral
1982	(June 21) First son, William, born
1983	Diana's first tours of Australia, New Zealand, and Canada
1984	(September 15) Second son, Harry, born
1988	(March 10) Death of Major Hugh Lindsay
1992	(June 15) Andrew Morton's book *Diana: Her True Story* reveals how unhappy Diana has become
1992	(December 9) Announcement of Diana and Charles's separation
1993	(December) Diana partly withdraws from public life
1995	(November 20) Diana gives *Panorama* TV interview
1996	(August 28) Diana and Charles are divorced; Diana plans to resign as patron of over 100 charities, to devote more time to six
1997	(August 31) Diana killed in Paris car accident
1997	(September 6) Diana's funeral in London and burial at Althorp

Glossary

boarding school school that pupils live in during the school year

Books of Condolence special book that people can sign and write messages of sympathy in

bulimia nervosa (or bulimia) eating disorder (illness), often caused by a low opinion of oneself

celebrity well-known person, a star

civilian person who is not in the army, navy, or air force

Commonwealth an association of the United Kingdom and various other places in the world which were or are ruled by Britain

custody guardianship or care of children after a divorce

documentary TV or radio program about real-life events

formal ceremonial, or somewhat stiff (in behavior)

heir someone who will get a title, property, or money when the person who owns these dies

heir-apparent heir, no matter who else might be born later

icon someone whose public image is almost worshiped

intrusive prying into someone's private life

media plural of medium (of communication), for example, newspapers, magazines, TV, radio

monarchy kind of government in which there is a monarch (a king or queen)

mourn feel great sadness when someone has died

mourner person who feels great sadness when someone has died

Parliament elected people who make the laws of a country

patron someone, usually well known, who gives official support to a good cause

pomp splendid display

Press Complaints Commission watchdog body to which people can complain about newspaper stories that offend them

press secretary someone who talks to reporters on behalf of his or her employer

role part to play, a job

syndication act of publishing something in several newspapers at once

speculated made guesses

tapped secretly listened to

upper class people with special titles and sometimes a lot of land and money

Windsor family name of Britain's monarchs since 1917

walkabout public event where someone royal meets the people in an informal, easy-going way

More Books to Read

Bach, Julie S. Princess *Diana*. Minneapolis, MN: Abdo & Daughters. 1991.

Licata, Renora. *Princess Diana: Royal Ambassador.* Danbury, CT: Blackbirch Press. 1993.

Wood, Richard. *Diana: The People's Princess.* Chatham, NJ: Raintree Steck-Vaughn. 1997.

INDEX